Original title:
Mellow Twigs Inside the Mermaid Cuff

Author: Swan Charm
ISBN HARDBACK: 978-1-80562-917-7
ISBN PAPERBACK: 978-1-80564-438-5

Crystallized Lustre of Forgotten Isles

In the mist where whispers dance,
Secrets lie, a fleeting glance.
Crystals formed from ocean's tears,
Guarding tales of ancient years.

Waves of time, they gently sway,
In shadows past, the dreams play.
Fragments of a world once bright,
Glimmer soft in fading light.

Chromatic Shadows on the Horizon

A palette vast, the sky ignites,
Colors clash in swirling flights.
Shadows stretch and merge with gold,
Stories new, yet ancient told.

The sun dips low, a gentle sigh,
Reflecting hues that kiss the sky.
Each hue holds a whispered plea,
Of hopes and dreams yet to be free.

Paintings of the Ocean's Tender Kiss

Brushstrokes wave on canvas blue,
An artist's heart, forever true.
The ocean speaks in tender tones,
In every ripple, life enthrones.

Seashells echo stories old,
In whispers soft, their secrets told.
Each crest and trough, a song of lore,
Of lovers lost on distant shore.

Dance of the Sirens' Solitude

In twilight's glow, their voices soar,
A melody from ocean's core.
Sirens spin in graceful plight,
Wrapped in shadows, cloaked in light.

Alone they weave their haunting song,
Enticing dreams where hearts belong.
Yet in their dance, a longing stays,
For whispered love that time betrays.

Shattered Glass of the Nautical Heart

In the depths where shadows dwell,
Glass fragments whisper tales to tell.
With every crash, a story breaks,
A sailor's dream, the sea awake.

Reflections dance on waters wide,
Memories lost, yet never died.
Each shard glimmers with hope's embrace,
Lost loves drift in that vast space.

Tides pull at the anchor deep,
Unraveled hearts begin to weep.
Yet in the storm, a beauty glows,
A fragile heart that still knows.

Beneath the surface, secrets sigh,
Of sailor's songs and lullabies.
They weave a net of silver spun,
Where fractured dreams and wishes run.

So gaze upon the ocean's glass,
Where every moment, fleeting, passes.
In shattered beauty, find the spark,
The nautical heart, once more, embarks.

Layers of Light Beneath the Waves

In whispered realms where silence reigns,
Light filters down through watery veins.
Layers of hue, a dancer's grace,
Each ray discovers a hidden place.

Coral castles, secrets kept,
In hues of pink where mermaids wept.
Bubbles rise like dreams set free,
A tapestry of mystery.

With every sinking heart, a glow,
Waves embrace what we don't know.
Voices thrill in currents strong,
An underwater, timeless song.

The depths hold stories, soft and clear,
Of whispered wishes held so dear.
Among the tides, we drift and sway,
The light reveals, and shadows play.

So dive into the ocean vast,
Where layers whisper of the past.
In every shimmer, magic lies,
Beneath the waves, our spirits rise.

The Poetry of a Shimmering Abyss

In the heart of darkness, flickers light,
A shimmering wish, a silent flight.
The abyss cradles dreams untold,
In swirls of azure, mysteries unfold.

Fathoms deep, where few have trod,
The ocean hums, a sacred nod.
Ink-blue depths with secrets steep,
Whispers of sorrow, wishes to keep.

Stars emerge from shadowed threads,
An alien love that language spreads.
With every pulse of the hollow night,
The essence of hope ignites the fight.

In currents swift, the heart shall roam,
Amongst the mermaids, finding home.
Eclipsed by depths where shadows sigh,
The poetry sings, and troubles die.

So listen close, the deep will speak,
Of shimmering dreams for the brave, the meek.
In hallowed silence, let it flow,
For in the abyss, our spirits glow.

Secrets in the Shimmering Surf

In the hush of twilight's call,
Waves whisper secrets to the shore,
Dreams entwined with cresting tides,
Mysteries lost at ocean's core.

Footprints vanish, swept away,
Echoes linger, soft and shy,
Shells and stories fill the sand,
Where the curious hearts roam high.

Glistening like stars that fall,
The moonlight merges with the foam,
Guiding sailors on their quest,
To find the path that leads them home.

Crabs skitter in a dance so light,
While dolphins leap with joyful grace,
The surf holds tales of day and night,
In every wave, a new embrace.

Secrets tinted with the salt,
Each splash reveals a silent song,
In the heart of endless tides,
The ocean's love is deep and strong.

Twirls of Sea Glass and Stardust

Underneath the shimmering waves,
Fragments of dreams gently collide,
A swirl of colors, soft and bright,
Where sea glass dances with the tide.

Each piece tells a tale of time,
Worn smooth by whispers of the sea,
Twinkling like stars in twilight's glow,
A treasure trove of memory.

With every twist, a story sings,
Murmured secrets held quite dear,
In the hands of fate, they glimmer,
As laughter bounces, loud and clear.

Twirling like wishes on the breeze,
They beckon from the ocean's floor,
A dance of stardust, wild and free,
Inviting us to explore once more.

In the ebb and flow of the night,
Where dreams drift on silken beams,
We find our place in the twilight glow,
Amongst the fragments of our dreams.

Soft Shadows in a Watercolor World

In the gentle brush of dawn's first light,
Colors blend as day breaks free,
Soft shadows creep, then melt away,
Painting life on a vibrant sea.

With splashes of turquoise and gold,
The canvas breathes, alive with grace,
Whispers of beauty, softly told,
In this enchanting, dreamlike place.

A watercolor world unconfined,
Where every hue can dance and play,
With strokes of joy, the heart entwined,
As nature sings in a sweet ballet.

Clouds drift like thoughts upon the sky,
Their shadows hint at tales long past,
Each petal sways, and time slips by,
In this realm of colors vast.

Life moves like ripples on a pond,
Soft shadows weaving through the day,
In a watercolor wonderland,
Where dreams and memories gently sway.

A Dance of Fragrant Tides

The tide comes in, a fragrant breeze,
Carrying whispers of the sea,
Seashell songs and blooms of salt,
In nature's dance, so wild and free.

With each wave that kisses the shore,
A rhythm flows, an ancient art,
A symphony of scents and sounds,
That stirs the deepest, hidden heart.

Driftwood sways in sunset's glow,
The ocean hums a lullaby,
As fireflies flicker, dance, and twirl,
Embracing dusk that stretches nigh.

Coconut, jasmine, and ocean air,
Blend together in fragrant light,
A perfume of the world's delight,
Under stars that shine so bright.

As tides retreat to gather strength,
They beckon dreams that long to glide,
In the dance of fragrant tides,
We find the magic deep inside.

Blushing Skies Over Rippled Waters

In twilight's glow, the heavens bloom,
With shades of rose, dispelling gloom.
The ripples dance on waters wide,
A canvas bright, where dreams abide.

The whispers soft from evening's breath,
Tell tales of love, and fleeting death.
Each star a wish, in velvet sky,
Reflecting hopes that soar and fly.

With every wave, a secret spun,
As night descends, the magic's begun.
The world anew, embraced in mist,
Where shadows play, and fairies twist.

Beneath the blush, the waters sigh,
As ancient tales of time slip by.
In sacred hush, the spirits glide,
Unraveling wonders, far and wide.

Ocean Treasures Wrapped in Silence

Beneath the tide, in depths profound,
Lie secrets kept, yet to be found.
A treasure chest where silence reigns,
With shimmering gems, and forgotten chains.

The whispered tales in currents flow,
Of sailors lost, and stars aglow.
Each coral branch, a history told,
Of voyages brave, and hearts bold.

In moonlit depths, the shadows blend,
Each undulating dream, a silent friend.
The ocean sings, but only to few,
Revealing worlds, both old and new.

Time's gentle hand caresses sand,
As echoes linger, a ghostly band.
The ocean's heart, a thumping beat,
Where silence wraps the world in sheets.

The Unseen Dance of Nautical Dreams

In the shroud of dusk, where dreams take flight,
The ocean sways in blissful night.
Unseen forces, the currents tease,
A dance of shadows, a breath of breeze.

The ships that sail on ghostly trails,
Whisper of legends, forgotten tales.
With every crest and trough they glide,
In harmony with the moon's soft tide.

The stars above, a guiding light,
To mariners lost in the folds of night.
Echoes of laughter, a siren's call,
In dreams entwined, they rise and fall.

A tapestry woven with whispers low,
As hearts set sail on the undertow.
The unseen dance, a cosmic play,
Where nautical dreams find their way.

Fables Carved in Driftwood Stories

On weathered shores, where driftwood sleeps,
Lie stories buried, the ocean keeps.
Each splintered piece, a tale untold,
Of heroes bold, and love grown cold.

The waves recite with rhythmic grace,
The echoes of time, a fleeting trace.
In every grain, a memory lives,
Of sunlight shared, and the tide that gives.

The hands that shape the wood so fine,
Create a world where dreams align.
With whispers soft as the sea breeze,
These fables linger, like drifting leaves.

As twilight falls, the stories surge,
From depths of heart, and ocean's verge.
Together they weave, a tapestry bright,
Of driftwood tales in the hush of night.

Timelessness Beneath the Surface

In the depths where shadows swell,
Whispers of the ages dwell,
Hidden tales in silence gleam,
Echoes of the forgotten dream.

Rippling secrets, soft and clear,
Every fragment holds a year,
Time unwinds in gentle streams,
Beneath the tides, the world redeems.

Waves embrace, and secrets flow,
Carried by the undertow,
Moments lost and moments gained,
In the depths, no heart is strained.

Where the moonlight sweeps the sand,
Ancient visions take a stand,
Fishes dart like fleeting thought,
In this realm, all time is caught.

Forgotten dreams, a tender bond,
Timeless rhythms, love's respond,
In every layer, life unfolds,
A tapestry of stories told.

Floating Lanterns of Seashell Night

Upon the sea, the lanterns gleam,
Floating softly, like a dream,
Nights adorned with gentle glow,
Whispers dance on tides below.

Seashells cradle hopes so bright,
As they sail through starry night,
Each a wish, a glinting spark,
Guided forth by winds so dark.

Carried forth on waves of grace,
Every lantern finds its place,
In the vast, the deep expanse,
Life unfolds in a sleepy trance.

Beneath the stars, their stories weave,
Silent dreams that we believe,
In the depths of ocean's heart,
All are given a brand-new start.

Floating by, the world feels light,
Hope and joy in seashell night,
Each glow a beacon, muzzled pain,
Guiding souls through sun and rain.

Swirls of Inconspicuous Beauty

In the shadows, colors blend,
Delicate hues that softly send,
Swirls of grace in quiet seams,
Life's unnoticed, gentle dreams.

Petals fall with whispered sighs,
In secret places, beauty lies,
Moments caught in fleeting flow,
Where no grand movements dare to show.

A dewdrop's glint, a quiet bloom,
In every nook, dispelling gloom,
Silent love in here and there,
Whispered breaths of tender care.

Nature's art, a mystic play,
In humble corners bright as day,
Life's patterns weave a soft array,
Innocent wonders, here they stay.

Setting suns, the twilight gleam,
In the shadows, visions beam,
Beauty hides in every crevice,
As the world remembers its bliss.

Ephemeral Patterns on Sandy Canvas

Where the ocean meets the shore,
Patterns tumble evermore,
Ephemeral trails in golden grains,
Stories etched that time remains.

Footprints of the wanderer's soul,
Each step a note, a distant toll,
Ebb and flow and gentle brush,
In the calm, the heart's sweet hush.

Waves that play a serenade,
Dance of light in shades that fade,
Moments crushed like shells so fine,
Every heartbeat, a whispered line.

Seagulls soar on evening's sigh,
Painting arcs against the sky,
Sandy canvas, a fleeting grace,
Each touch a love, a warm embrace.

As the tide brings forth its tale,
Shapes that vanish, dreams on sail,
In the sand, our footprints rest,
Ephemeral, yet truly blessed.

Crystal Reflections in Dappled Light

In the morning's gentle glow,
Dancing shards of light do play,
Like whispers of a secret world,
Beneath the leaves, they softly sway.

Rippling surfaces catch the sky,
Mirrored dreams in water's grace,
Every glint a fleeting thought,
In nature's quiet, sacred space.

The breeze does hum a mystic tune,
As sunlight skips from stone to stone,
Each crystal gleam, a fleeting gift,
In this forest realm, alone.

Petals fall, a soft embrace,
Cascading down, a vibrant rain,
They join the dance of light and shade,
In this ephemeral, sweet refrain.

Beneath the boughs where secrets lie,
Life's kaleidoscope unfurls anew,
With every step, the world awake,
In harmony, we find our view.

Threads of Melodies in a Tidal Pool

Among the rocks, the sea does sing,
A lullaby of salt and foam,
Each whisper woven through the waves,
In nature's heart, we call it home.

Shimmering stars in twilight's grasp,
Glimmer like pearls on a velvet stage,
Echoes twist through the ocean's breath,
As rhythmic tides mark every page.

Crabs dance in their tiny suits,
Shells adorn the sandy floor,
Each creature sings a subtle tune,
In the calm, where spirits soar.

Dappled light on water's skin,
Chants of sea entwined with air,
In this stillness, we find the notes,
Of life's grand, melodic prayer.

With every splash, the heart's desire,
To listen close and understand,
The symphony of waves that call,
To those who dream and seek the strand.

The Simplicity of Aquatic Whispers

Gentle sighs beneath the waves,
Rippling tales of ages past,
Each bubble takes a breath and floats,
A moment's joy, too quick to last.

In the depths, a silver flash,
A dance of fish, a fleeting glance,
They weave through sunlight, soft and sweet,
In liquid realms, they skip and prance.

The quiet murmur of the tide,
A language only few can know,
With secrets sung by silent stones,
The mysteries in currents flow.

A shell, a treasure from the deep,
Holds stories of the sea's embrace,
Each whisper cradles dreams untold,
In vulnerability, we trace.

Beneath the surface, worlds collide,
In symphony and stillness meld,
With each soft wave, a truth unveiled,
In gentle ripples, hearts are held.

Artifacts of Tide-touched Spa

Upon the shore, the treasures lie,
Driftwood, seashells, time in hand,
Each piece a chapter of the sea,
A history both vast and grand.

Washed by waves in twilight's glow,
Each artifact a whispered tale,
Of ships that sailed on distant seas,
And storms that wove their song to sail.

A polished stone, a wish upon,
Reflection caught in sunlit air,
The ocean's hand, forever moulds,
Its bounty blessed, beyond compare.

While children laugh, the gulls do cry,
Echoing dreams of days gone by,
Each tide reveals what time has shaped,
A canvas for the keenest eye.

In every grain, the essence holds,
The tides that ebb and flow with grace,
In nature's spa, our souls renew,
Embracing love, in every place.

The Soft Embrace of Changing Tides

In whispers soft, the ocean sighs,
A dance of light beneath the skies.
With every surge, a story weaves,
And dreams are born on salted leaves.

The moon ascends, a guiding eye,
As shadows drift, the currents fly.
A heartbeat syncs with ebb and flow,
In twilight's grasp, the waters glow.

The sands bear witness, tales of old,
Of sailors brave, and treasures told.
Where time stands still, the heart finds peace,
In nature's arms, sweet moments cease.

With every crest, the laughter swells,
In every wave, a secret dwells.
For tides that change, they bring and take,
An endless cycle, love's sweet wake.

The sea's embrace, a tender hold,
A timeless song that won't grow cold.
So let us tread where dreams abound,
In gentle tides, our hearts are found.

Whims of Waves and Waxing Moons

The moonlight dances on the tide,
In silken sheath, the stars collide.
With every wave, the night unfolds,
As whispers weave through stories told.

Beneath the sky, so vast and wide,
The ocean sings, a faithful guide.
The whims of waves, a playful twirl,
In lunar light, the waters swirl.

The sea reflects the dreams we share,
In moments fleeting, soft as air.
With every rise, a promise bends,
As whispers speak of love that mends.

The tides might change, but hearts remain,
In salty tears and joy, the same.
With waxing moon, our spirits soar,
Together lost on ocean shore.

So let us chase the azure flight,
With every wave, embrace the night.
For in the depths where memories bloom,
We find our light in gentle gloom.

Everlasting Tides of Serene Reflection

In quiet tides, the soul finds rest,
A mirrored calm, the heart's true quest.
Reflections dance on waters deep,
In tranquil moments, secrets keep.

The gentle sway of ocean's breath,
Whispers life amidst the death.
With every wave, a promise made,
In silent shores, our fears will fade.

The sands will shift, but here we stand,
A bond unbroken, hand in hand.
In every ripple, love's embrace,
An everlasting, sacred space.

The tides may turn, yet still we greet,
The ebb and flow, a rhythmic beat.
In serene reflections, we discover,
The endless circle, soul to lover.

So let the ocean sing its tune,
Under the watchful eye of moon.
For in the tides, our hearts align,
In timeless whispers, forever shine.

Waterscapes of Forgotten Memories

In waters deep where shadows dwell,
Forgotten tales, a whispered spell.
The currents swirl with time's embrace,
Unraveled dreams in a secret place.

With every splash, the past ignites,
A tapestry of lost delights.
In ripples clear, the echoes chime,
Of laughing voices lost to time.

The sea caresses with gentle touch,
A soothing balm, it means so much.
In salty breeze, the memories fly,
As tides of time will never die.

Sailors' songs in the twilight glow,
Throughout the years, their love will flow.
In waterscapes where memories blend,
We hold the stories, hearts to mend.

So wander forth by ocean's edge,
And hear the whispers, hear the pledge.
For in the depths of time's own sea,
Lie waterscapes of you and me.

The Fable of Sea Glass Shards

In the whispering shores where secrets glimmer,
Dreams dance like grains in the setting sun.
Each shard of glass tells a story of shimmer,
Of storms that raged and battles won.

Fragments of colors, a treasure reborn,
Glistening softly beneath azure skies.
Crafted by waves, washed and worn,
Reflecting the world through ancient eyes.

A sailor's journey, lost in the depth,
Seeking the beauty in life's every part.
With each tiny piece, a life is left,
A testament to the breaking heart.

So treasure these shards, and remember well,
Each color a tale, a spell to unfold.
In the depths of the sea, where mysteries dwell,
The fable of glass, a wonder retold.

From the depths, the sea whispers, not all is bleak,
There's magic in remnants, an echo divine.
Gather these shards, let your spirit speak,
For every piece holds a love so fine.

Reverie Among Coral Vines

In a garden where coral blooms bright,
Tangled vines weave through restless seas.
Beneath the waves, a magical sight,
Where hopes breathe softly with every breeze.

Little fish dart like whispers of light,
Among the tendrils, a joyous ballet.
In this realm, where dusk surrenders to night,
A realm of colors, where dreams come to play.

The coral whispers secrets of old,
Of lovers lost in a dance of the deep.
Their stories echo, a treasure untold,
A lullaby for the ocean to keep.

Each wave a lull, each tide a new chance,
To sway with the currents of endless grace.
Among coral vines, let the heart take a dance,
In this world of wonder, a sacred place.

So rest within this marine embrace,
Where coral and dreams bloom evermore.
In the tapestry woven with gentle lace,
Find your reverie on the ocean's floor.

Lament of the Wandering Tide

Oh, wandering tide, with your restless heart,
You kiss the shores and sigh in despair.
Each ebb a farewell, a tear, a new start,
Yearning for land, though never quite there.

You carry the weight of the moon's soft pull,
Rising and falling, a dance of your fate.
Across the horizon, your whispers are full,
Of tales of longing, of love and of hate.

You cradle the shells, the treasures you find,
Silent witnesses to your endless roam.
Yet deep in your swell, lies a heart intertwined,
With echoes of laughter, forever to comb.

In the twilight hours, you murmur and wail,
A lull for the dreamers lost in the night.
As you weave through the stars, let your sorrow unveil,
Your lament a song, a bittersweet flight.

So sing to the oceans, oh tide that won't rest,
Enfold us in whispers, where dreams ride the swell.
For in your embrace lies both sorrow and jest,
A wandering tapestry, a story to tell.

Tranquil Currents of Sunlit Waters

In the stillness where sunlight meets deep,
Waters shimmer in hues of gold.
Amidst the reflections, the heart starts to leap,
In the cradle of calm, where secrets unfold.

Beneath the surface, the world's gentle sway,
Echoes the peace of the morning's first light.
Tranquil currents invite us to play,
Lulling the heart with their soothing delight.

The dance of the ripples, a soft serenade,
Caresses the shores with a tender embrace.
In each breath, the worries of life start to fade,
As time drifts like whispers in this sacred space.

Here in the waters, all troubles diminish,
A sanctuary where dreams never cease.
Embrace the current, let your spirit replenish,
In this tranquil realm, find your inner peace.

So dive into depths where wonder resides,
Amidst sunlit waters, your soul can take flight.
In the quiet embrace of the ebbing tides,
Seek the beauty within, and bask in the light.

Lullaby of the Fathomless Depths

Whispers of waves, a soft embrace,
Cradling secrets in their grace.
Beneath the moon's serene glow,
Dreams take flight, and currents flow.

Stars twinkle above, a distant song,
Lulling the night where shadows belong.
In ocean's heart, silence keeps,
Guarding the mysteries it softly weeps.

Gentle tides kiss the sandy shore,
Echoing tales of the depths and more.
A lullaby sung in whispered threads,
Where every ripple echoes the dead.

Dancing lights on the water's face,
Guide weary souls to a resting place.
With every swell, a promise made,
In fathomless depths where dreams are laid.

So drift away on the evening's breath,
Let the ocean cradle you past death.
For in its arms, the cycle spins,
And life begins where the darkness thins.

Fables of Gnarled Ocean Boughs

Once among the twisted roots,
Where sea meets wood, adventure shoots.
Legends whispered through the breeze,
Tales of ships, lost in seas.

With branches bent from storms and years,
They hold the laughter, the hopes, the tears.
A faded map to buried gold,
Secrets of sailors, brave and bold.

In shadows deep, where waters dwell,
The gnarled boughs weave a spell.
For every wave that crashes near,
Is a story told, a song to hear.

Ebbing tides and drifting sands,
Mark the journeys made by hands.
Once mighty vessels now decay,
But their fables live on in the spray.

So listen close to the ocean's call,
In twisted woods, where echoes fall.
For every branch holds ancient lore,
Of love and loss, forevermore.

Secrets Veiled in Liquid Hues

Deep in the depths, a canvas swirls,
With every ripple, a story unfurls.
Secrets cloaked in aquamarine,
Whispers of things that have never been.

The tides hold visions, both bright and dark,
Mirrored memories where shadows spark.
Liquid hues dance in twilight's glow,
Carving the tales of the ebb and flow.

In twilight waters where silence reigns,
Hidden emotions stir like chains.
For every color a pulse, a sigh,
And secrets linger where dreams might lie.

Within the depths, where light can't creep,
Visions of wonders, forever keep.
A cradle of echoes, deep and wide,
Veiled in liquid, where dreams abide.

So dive into the depths unknown,
Where vibrant whispers lead you home.
For life unfolds in subtler hues,
And magic waits in the ocean's muse.

The Enigma of Driftwood Dreams

On shores where whispers kiss the sand,
Driftwood lies, a sculptor's hand.
Each twisted piece holds time's embrace,
Stories crafted in nature's grace.

With sun-bleached bark and ocean's stain,
A testament to beauty gained.
In every groove, a myth resides,
Of travelers lost on endless tides.

Beneath the stars, they softly gleam,
Dreams of sailors beneath the seam.
Salt and wood, a fragrant blend,
A journey's start or a tale's end.

And every driftwood, a life reborn,
Whispering secrets in the morn.
In quiet corners of moonlit shores,
Where thrumming heart and ocean roars.

So gather 'round, let the tales unfold,
Of driftwood dreams, both brave and bold.
For in their arms, the past still sighs,
An enigma wrapped in gentle lies.

Cradled by the Salted Breeze

Upon the shore where seagulls cry,
The waves whisper tales to the night sky.
Fingers of foam, lace the ancient sand,
In the salty air, dreams wander and stand.

Beneath the moon's glow, shadows dance light,
Each breeze carries secrets, out of our sight.
With every gust, the ocean sighs,
As stars blink awake in the vast, dark highs.

Hope wades in waters that shimmer and sway,
Where the heart finds solace at the close of day.
Each grain of salt, a story untold,
Of mysteries wrapped in blue and gold.

Cradled by nature, I breathe the sea,
In the arms of the tide, I am forever free.
The shores may shift, but my spirit's tied,
To the rhythms of waves, where my dreams abide.

The salted breeze, a soft embrace,
Whispers of love in this sacred place.
In every gust, a chant of the wild,
Where time stands still, and the heart's a child.

Hidden Currents of Calm

In the depths of the sea, where silence reigns,
Hidden currents weave quiet lanes.
A tapestry spun of tranquil dreams,
Where the mind drifts softly, or so it seems.

Beneath the surface, harmony swirls,
Magic lies waiting, in spirals and twirls.
Gentle hands of fate guide the flow,
Through the shadows where secrets grow.

Yet in the quiet, the heart beats strong,
In the hush of the depths, where I belong.
Each ripple carries a hint of grace,
In these hidden realms, I find my place.

Waves whisper softly of hopes anew,
Promises held in the ocean's blue.
With every pulse, the calm unfolds,
Stories of courage in depths untold.

Here, beneath the weight of the sky,
I dance with the currents as they pass by.
In the embrace of the deep, I remain,
Among the treasures where stillness reigns.

The Empress of Dusk and Depths

Amidst twilight whispers, she rules divine,
The Empress of dusk, where shadows entwine.
In her gaze, the horizon blushes bright,
As day slowly surrenders to night.

Her crown of stars, a shimmering grace,
Each light a reflection of time and space.
With waves as her subjects, she calls them near,
In the hush of twilight, her voice is clear.

Draped in twilight, her kingdom expands,
Where the depths of the ocean embrace the sands.
Her heart beats with rhythms of the deep,
As creatures of twilight begin to leap.

In her realm, dreams are spun like thread,
Weaving tales of magic that wander ahead.
The dusk showcases her regal flair,
Calling forth wonders that float in the air.

She paints the sky with colors of dusk,
As secrets emerge from the ocean's husk.
In the depths where her essence thrives,
Empress of twilight, where magic survives.

Shapes of Nautical Harmony

In the weave of the sea, shapes take flight,
Dancing through shadows, embracing the light.
Each wave a note in the ocean's song,
Creating a symphony, harmonious and strong.

Sailboats drift in the lull of the breeze,
Gliding with grace, as the heart finds ease.
In the spray of the water, joy intertwines,
As the spirits of sailors weave through the pines.

Stars gleam above in celestial embrace,
Guiding the lost to a familiar place.
In the patterns of waves, life finds its way,
Through undulating rhythms, come night or day.

Shapes of tranquility carved by the tide,
Render the secrets that nature can't hide.
Each crest, a whisper of dreams left behind,
In the deep, there's a language unconfined.

Together they flow, earth, sea, and sky,
In nautical harmony, they rise and fly.
In the heart of the ocean, peace takes its stand,
As life dances lightly on the grains of sand.

A Song of Shell and Shore

Upon the beach where sea foam plays,
The shells do sing of ancient days.
With whispers soft, they tell their tale,
Of ships and storms, of wind and sail.

The tides roll in with gentle grace,
Each wave a memory, time can't erase.
The sun dips low, the sky aglow,
In twilight's arms, the sea winds blow.

The sand lies warm, a lover's touch,
While seagulls cry, their wings a hush.
Footprints marred by ocean's sweep,
The secrets of the shore, they keep.

Beneath the stars, the waters gleam,
A lullaby drifts like a dream.
The shells whisper love, loss, and lore,
In every grain, the heart can soar.

So grab a shell, hold it near,
Let its music fill your ear.
For by the shore, on every quest,
The sea's own song shall grant you rest.

Rustic Whispers of the Waves

In quiet nooks where rivers bend,
The waves weave tales, old as time.
With rustic charm, they softly send,
A melody that feels like rhyme.

Beneath the boughs of willow trees,
Where sunbeams dance on rippling foam,
The gentle current's sweet decrees
Make every heart feel like its home.

The stones are smooth, the air is clear,
Each splash a note of nature's score.
In every echo, close and near,
The water hums what came before.

With every tide, the land will change,
Yet whispers of the past remain.
Though seasons shift, and winds rearrange,
The waves will sing in joy or pain.

So linger long by rustic banks,
Let thoughts drift like the floating leaves.
For in the waves, the spirit thanks
The silent power that never leaves.

Mysteries of Tidal Caverns

Deep in the cliffs, where shadows dwell,
The tidal caverns hide their lore.
Each echo whispers, like a spell,
Of ancient secrets, tales of yore.

The water dances, dark and deep,
As moonlight filters through the stone.
In stillness wrapped, the ancients sleep,
And time forgets what once was known.

With nimble steps, we venture on,
Into the heart of nature's might.
In every wave, a forgotten song,
In every crack, a glimmering light.

The salty breeze, a ghostly friend,
Calls forth the thoughts beneath the waves.
These caverns hold what will not end,
The mysteries that the sea engraves.

So let us wander, hearts aflame,
In tidal realms, where whispers flow.
For every cavern holds a name,
In every tide, the world will glow.

Gentle Mists in an Aquatic Dream

When dawn awakes with softest sighs,
And mists hang low upon the lake,
The world transforms with veiled surprise,
In gentle hues, the spirits wake.

The water shimmers, calm and bright,
Reflecting dreams from night's embrace.
In tranquil waves, there's pure delight,
A moment caught in time and space.

With every ripple, stories spin,
Of whispered thoughts and secrets shared.
In liquid depths, where dreams begin,
The essence of the heart is bared.

So close your eyes and breathe it in,
The mist, a cloak, so soft, so sweet.
For in this dream, new worlds begin,
Where aquatic wonders, softly meet.

Let currents guide you, lost yet found,
In dreams where water holds its throes.
For in this place, on magic ground,
The gentle mists entwine like prose.

Siren's Call Amidst Flora's Grasp

In the cradle of green, whispers weave,
Where the petals sway, magic believes.
A song of the siren, sweet and clear,
Pulls at the heartstrings, drawing near.

Amidst the wild blooms, shadows dance,
Echoes of laughter, a haunting trance.
With every note, the forest sighs,
As the breeze carries secrets, through the skies.

Under moonlight's gaze, a dream unfurls,
Guided by starlight, through hidden swirls.
Nature and melody, hand in hand,
Lost in a world, exquisitely planned.

Roots twist and twine, binding the deep,
While the sirens sing what the wild hearts keep.
Between the sagas of flora's embrace,
Lie tales of longing, in every place.

So heed the call, where enchantments bloom,
In a world where echoes dissolve the gloom.
For amidst the flora, a siren's tale,
Awaits in the whispers, riding the gale.

Tapestry of Seafoam and Shadows

Upon the shore, where sea meets sand,
Waves weave stories, both fated and grand.
In foamy lace, the secrets lie,
Crafted by tides that murmur and sigh.

Moonlight glistens, a silvery thread,
Binding the dark where shadows tread.
Each crest and trough holds whispers of old,
In the tapestry woven, tales unfold.

Gulls cry above, like voices of mist,
Calling the dreamers to join the tryst.
With salt on their lips, they long to explore,
The depths of the ocean, forevermore.

Yet danger lurks in the shimmering foam,
A call to adventure, a journey home.
In the heart of the tempest, courage arises,
As lovers meet, each moment surprises.

So gather 'round, where the waters dance,
In the embrace of fate, the daring glance.
For in every wave and every shadow cast,
A lifetime of dreams is knit to the past.

Melodies of Water's Embrace

In the heart of the glen, where whispers flow,
A symphony swells, soft and low.
With each gentle ripple, a note takes flight,
Sung by the water, bathed in light.

The brook sings sweetly, a lullaby clear,
Crooning to willow and birch standing near.
Threads of crystal and silver entwine,
Creating a melody, timeless and fine.

Amidst the rushes, the songbirds reply,
Their voices entwined, a choir on high.
In the dance of the leaves, they pirouette sweet,
Merging with whispers of water's heartbeat.

Dawn paints the skies, a canvas aglow,
While dreams drift softly upon waves below.
With every soft splash, stories start anew,
In melodies woven with morning's dew.

So linger awhile, let the cadence surround,
In the echoes of water, a harmony found.
As the world fades away, and peace takes its place,
In the heart of the glen, find your solace and grace.

Reflections in the Shimmering Tide

In the quiet dusk, where the waters gleam,
Shadows dance lightly, caught in a dream.
Mirrored reflections of stars and skies,
Glimmer in whispers, as twilight sighs.

As the ocean breathes, secrets arise,
Tales of the moon, lost in her eyes.
Each ripple a story, woven in time,
Echoing softly, in rhythm and rhyme.

Sails on the horizon, shifting and bold,
Chasing the sunset, glimmers of gold.
In the embrace of the night's cool grace,
Shores of remembrance, a comforting place.

A lull of the tide, a soft, gentle lull,
Waves whisper words, that beckon the soul.
In twilight's embrace, where dreams intertwine,
The shimmer of water reveals a design.

So gaze at the sea, where reflections reside,
And listen to stories, as currents confide.
For in the soft glow, magic is found,
In the shimmering tide, where love knows no bound.

Light Weaving Through Obsidian Water

In depths where shadows dance and play,
The glints of silver twist and sway.
They weave a tale of starry night,
That flickers faint in soft moonlight.

Each ripple sings a whispered song,
Of currents deep and realms long gone.
Where secrets dwell beneath the foam,
And dreams of wanderers find a home.

The light, a brush on velvet dark,
Can summon hope, ignite a spark.
With every wave, the heartbeats race,
As echoes flicker in the space.

The obsidian keeps time concealed,
A canvas showing what's revealed.
In every depth, a mystery,
A tapestry of history.

So let us dive, let shadows guide,
To where the wondrous worlds reside.
And when the dawn breaks through the night,
We'll rise above, our hearts alight.

Murmurs of the Shell Collector

Upon the shore where driftwood sleeps,
He roams, collecting secrets, keeps.
Every shell tells stories spun,
Of tides and storms, of lost and won.

He bends to hear the ocean's sigh,
A fragile whisper, a lullaby.
With every treasure held in hand,
A universe at his command.

The colors swirl, the patterns loom,
A gallery born from sea's own womb.
In hues of twilight, shadows blend,
Each shell a token, a cherished friend.

Yet in the swirling sands, a call,
For all the shells, he must let fall.
For nature sings, and with each wave,
A lesson learned, a soul to save.

With every find, he learns to feel,
The fragile hearts that time can heal.
In murmurs soft, the oceans tell,
Of life and love, and lost farewell.

Petals Under the Celestial Tide

Beneath the stars, where dreamers weave,
In depths of night, the hearts believe.
Petals drift on whispers soft,
Carried by winds, aloft, aloft.

Each bloom unveils a tale of grace,
In lunar glow, they find their place.
As silver water meets the shore,
A symphony, forevermore.

The tides embrace, the petals spin,
A dance beneath the twilight's skin.
Each gentle wave, a lover's sigh,
As time slips by, and dreams all fly.

In colors rich, a canvas bright,
Of love and loss, beneath the night.
The petals whisper long-forgotten,
In the tide's embrace, all weary, trodden.

So let them drift, let them unfold,
Stories in waves, both brave and bold.
For under the sky, where beauty hides,
Petals whisper softly with the tides.

Flourish of Seafoam Colors

In bursts of foam, the colors blend,
A canvas rich on which dreams send.
The sun ignites the ocean's face,
In hues of joy, a warm embrace.

With every wave, a story swells,
Of ancient seas and hidden wells.
In emerald greens and sapphire blues,
The water spins its mystic hues.

The laughter of the waves does sing,
A merry tune that makes hearts spring.
While sea birds dive and dance above,
A flourish bright, as if in love.

Each splash a burst of nature's art,
That makes a joyful, tender heart.
The tides reflect each fleeting glance,
A world submerged in ocean dance.

So let us cherish these vibrant waves,
In their embrace, our spirit saves.
For in this seafoam, we are whole,
A vivid splash within the soul.

Ripples Under Silver Moonlight

A silver gaze upon the stream,
Whispers of night weave through the dream.
Stars waltz lightly in the sky,
As gentle echoes draw a sigh.

The water dances, shimmer bright,
Unfolding secrets, pure delight.
Caught in time, the moment sways,
Beneath the moon's soft, soothing rays.

A lullaby of tranquil night,
Wraps around the heart so tight.
Ripples chorus, sweet and round,
In this magic, peace is found.

The trees lean close, in shadows deep,
Guarding secrets they all keep.
Brightened dreams in twilight's glow,
As silver waves begin to flow.

Nature hums a soft refrain,
Embracing life with soft champagne.
The world holds its breath, aglow,
While ripples waltz, and time moves slow.

Drifted Echoes of Enchanted Waters

From depths where magic does reside,
Drifted echoes in dreams collide.
The waters weave a tale retold,
Of mysteries, both brave and bold.

Beneath the swirl of shadows cast,
Ancient whispers from the past.
Tales of hope and hidden fears,
Float like petals kissed by tears.

Rippling currents hum a tune,
Beneath the watchful, pale full moon.
Waves that carry tales of yore,
Sing of dreams from distant shore.

Drifted echoes softly sigh,
In the twilight, whispers fly.
Crystals glimmer, reflecting light,
Enchanted waters bless the night.

With every pulse, a heart takes flight,
In the kingdom of starry white.
Flowing gently, time unwinds,
Steeped in lace of magic binds.

A Fable of Coral Dawn

As dawn arrives with tender grace,
A coral blush paints every face.
The sea awakens with a sigh,
Beneath the vast and waking sky.

Waves of whispered tales arise,
Hopeful dreams, like birds, they fly.
Coral reefs in morning's glow,
Guarding treasures down below.

Beneath the waves, a world unfolds,
In hues of blue and softest gold.
Echoes of life, both fierce and free,
Dance to the rhythm of the sea.

A melody of soft embrace,
Nature's love, a warm embrace.
With every tide, a story spun,
In the light of the waking sun.

Awake the dreams of ocean's heart,
Where every creature plays a part.
A fable whispered through the waves,
In coral dawn, the magic braves.

Breezes Through Weathered Waterways

Breezes wander, free and light,
Through weathered pathways, out of sight.
They carry tales from far away,
Of loves and losses, night and day.

The rivers flow with stories old,
Of daring hearts and dreams so bold.
Each bend and turn a secret keeps,
As whispers rise from ancient deeps.

Through tangled roots and mossy trails,
Breezes lift forgotten sails.
They dance upon the surface bright,
In harmony with fading light.

Embers flicker, shadows blend,
Where time and water gently mend.
Each ripple sings of days gone by,
A tapestry beneath the sky.

So follow breezes, heed their call,
Through weathered waterways, we'll all
Find echoes of what used to be,
With every turn, adventure free.

Portraits of the Ebbing Heart

In twilight's glow, the shadows dance,
Each flicker holds a wistful glance.
The memories wrapped in whispered sighs,
Like fleeting stars in velvet skies.

With every heartbeat, tales unfold,
Of love, of loss, of secrets told.
From painted lips to distant shores,
The ebbing heart forever explores.

Time's canvas stretches, colors fade,
Yet in our hearts, the hues are laid.
Reflections deep, a silent call,
A tapestry that binds us all.

In corners dark, where dreams retreat,
The pulse of hope, a steady beat.
With courage wrapped in soft despair,
Each portrait breathes a whispered prayer.

So linger not on shadows cast,
Embrace the echoes of the past.
For every heart that's ever wept,
Holds tales of joy, of love, of depth.

The Rugged Elegance of Ocean Stones

Upon the shore where water meets,
The ocean whispers, softly greets.
Each stone unique, a tale of old,
In rugged grace, their beauty bold.

The tides bestow a gentle kiss,
While seagulls cry their songs of bliss.
Embracing all that life has won,
In frothy waves, their dance begun.

We walk among their polished dreams,
With every step, their laughter streams.
A symphony of earth and sea,
In every stone, a mystery.

Beneath the sun, their colors flare,
Greens and blues, a painter's dare.
Each grain of sand, a world of cheer,
In rugged elegance, we appear.

The whispering winds, like voices known,
In nature's arms, we are not alone.
For every stone that graces the shore,
Holds stories vast, forevermore.

Jewelry of the Depths at Rest

In twilight depths where shadows twine,
Lie treasures bright, both rare and fine.
Necklaces spun from moonlit beams,
Jewelry of dreams, lost in streams.

The currents hum a gentle tune,
Each glimmer sings beneath the moon.
Emerald greens and sapphire blues,
Crafted by time, in whispers, fuse.

Forgotten relics, time's embrace,
Drifting softly in their place.
The ocean's heart, a treasure chest,
Where silent stories find their rest.

Beneath the waves, in freedom's flight,
Glimmers of hope shine soft and bright.
Each pearl a wish, a love confessed,
Jewelry of the depths, at rest.

So let us dive in dreams profound,
To seek the treasures lost, yet found.
In ocean's arms, our souls take wing,
To hear the songs the ancients sing.

Laced Memories of the Salted Breeze

The salted breeze, a gentle sigh,
Whispers secrets as it passes by.
Wrapped in lace, the stories swirl,
Of distant lands, where dreams unfurl.

With every breath, the ocean speaks,
Of summer days and sun-kissed weeks.
Each gust a kiss from faraway shores,
Where laughter lingers, and spirit soars.

In twilight's glow, the horizon gleams,
A canvas painted with lovers' dreams.
Laced with promises, soft and sweet,
The salted breeze, a lover's heartbeat.

As twilight deepens, shadows play,
In silken waves, we drift away.
For in the air, the past resides,
In laced memories, the heart abides.

So let us dance 'neath the silver moon,
To the salty breeze's timeless tune.
With open hearts, we'll chase the night,
In woven dreams, we find our light.

A Dance Beneath the Whispering Waves

Beneath the waves, a dance does twirl,
Mermaids weave with laughter's swirl.
In moonlit glades, where secrets sigh,
Their voices float, a lullaby.

The seafoam glimmers, pearls do gleam,
In silver light, they craft a dream.
A world of wonders, lost and found,
In ocean's heart, where magic's bound.

The tides do rise, the tides do fall,
As shadows play on coral's wall.
With every splash, a tale unfolds,
Of ancient myths and treasures bold.

In whispered winds, a sailor's fate,
Guided by stars, as they await.
The rhythm calls, a siren's song,
Where every heart will find its throng.

So dance, dear child, beneath the sky,
With dreams as vast as waves that sigh.
For in this twirl of sea and light,
The world is yours, hold it tight.

Ethereal Echoes in a Coastal Cradle

In coastal cradles, echoes play,
Whispers of dusk and dawn's ballet.
The shoreline sings, with every wave,
A lullaby, inviting the brave.

With breezes soft, like gentle hands,
They shape the dreams upon the sands.
Each shell a story, bright and fair,
Of lovers lost and burdens rare.

The gulls take flight, a joyous choir,
As sunsets paint the sky with fire.
In twilight's glow, the sea rides high,
A dance of hues, where wishes lie.

In secret tides, the heart will roam,
Finding a spirit's ancient home.
The ebb and flow, a timeless grace,
A journey stitched in lace and space.

So linger here, where dreams unfold,
In coastal cradles, tales are told.
Let echoes lead your heart anew,
In waves of whispers, find what's true.

Hidden Hearts of Pebble Shores

Upon the shores of pebbles fine,
Hidden hearts in silence twine.
Each stone a secret, waiting long,
To share its tale in nature's song.

With every step, a whisper stirs,
Of ancient paths and quiet purrs.
The tide's embrace, a soft caress,
Unveils the past, a lover's press.

Beneath the moon's enchanting glow,
The pebbles glisten, tales in tow.
They held the footsteps of the brave,
And wove the dreams the nightwaves crave.

In quiet nooks, the heart will find,
A peace that binds, a place that's kind.
Amongst the stones, connections flow,
As timeless as the waves that go.

So wander here, where whispers creep,
In hidden hearts, your wishes keep.
For on these shores, the stories blend,
In pebble's heart, the journey's end.

Celestial Whirls and Ocean Pearls

In celestial whirls, the heavens spin,
Where ocean pearls meet dusk's soft grin.
With every wave, a star descends,
In cosmic dance, where magic bends.

The tides reflect the night's embrace,
A twinkling smile on salt-kissed face.
As starlit dreams drift through the air,
The sea recalls the worlds laid bare.

With every splash, a secret told,
Of treasures deep, both new and old.
Celestial realms in water's flow,
Where moonlight mingles with ebb and glow.

In cosmic currents, hearts collide,
With whispers sweet, the stars reside.
The ocean's depth, a vast expanse,
Where dreams and destiny advance.

So dive into this realm so wide,
With every pearl, let hope abide.
In celestial whirls, your soul entwined,
In ocean's heart, true joy you'll find.

Mossy Hues of Forgotten Shores

Upon the shore where secrets lie,
Moss clings to stones, a gentle sigh.
Whispers of waves in twilight's embrace,
Time turns slow in this hallowed space.

Old tales drift on the salty breeze,
Carried by currents amongst the trees.
Footprints of dreams in the soft wet sand,
Each one a story, a fleeting strand.

Golden shells gleam from the ocean's kiss,
Marking the hours that we dare to miss.
Beneath the green where wildflowers bloom,
Lies a world wrapped in a fragrant gloom.

Secrets unfold in the cool sea air,
Echoes of laughter, a child's fair prayer.
Nature's canvas, in colors of time,
Brush strokes of memory, vivid, sublime.

As the sun dips low, a fire ignites,
Painting the waves in soft, golden lights.
Mossy hues cradle the end of day,
In silence, the night bids the light to stay.

Gossamer Threads of Ocean Lullabies

Beneath the moon where the soft waves play,
Lullabies murmur, inviting the day.
Gossamer dreams drift on silken foam,
Carried by tides that call us home.

Stars flicker softly, a shimmering show,
Dancing like whispers, a gentle glow.
Each note of water, a sweet serenade,
Guiding lost souls through the twilight's shade.

Seafarers' tales, spun in the night,
Wrapped in the mist, lost to our sight.
Voices of sirens blend with the breeze,
Casting a spell that time few can seize.

With every ripple, the heart dreams wide,
Drifting through realms on an ocean's tide.
Gossamer threads weave us to the light,
Cradling hopes as they take to flight.

As dawn's first breath upon the waves breaks,
Magic lingers where the ocean wakes.
Each lullaby holds a secret untold,
In the depths of the sea, treasures unfold.

Tides of Serene Enchantment

In quiet hues where the waters meet,
Tides of enchantment weave soft and sweet.
Whispers of coral, a dancer's grace,
Beneath the surface, a hidden place.

Seashells gather in clusters of gold,
Stories of sailors and myths of old.
The sea's calm heart beats steadily,
A rhythm that carries, wild and free.

On windswept dunes, the grasses sway,
Echoing tales that the ocean may say.
Ripples of laughter, serene and bright,
Merge with the stars as they guard the night.

Each tide that rises, a promise to keep,
Woven in dreams that the ancients reap.
In the shell's soft curve, secrets abide,
Callback to moments the heart cannot hide.

As dusk's soft cloak wraps the world in peace,
Nature's symphony offers release.
In tides of magic, we find our way,
Bathed in enchantment, come what may.

Selkie's Embrace in Twilight Mist

In twilight's mist where shadows dance,
The selkie glimmers, a fleeting glance.
Seaweed spirals, a silken embrace,
Hiding her laughter in ocean's grace.

With every ripple, secrets unfurl,
Whispering wonders of the deep world.
Stars weave their tales in the dusk's cool breath,
Guiding lost souls on the edge of death.

In the moonlight's glow, she sings of old,
Her voice a treasure, a magic untold.
Each haunting note tugs at the heart,
Binding the weary with love's gentle art.

The waves curl softly, like arms open wide,
Inviting the lonely to cast aside pride.
Wrapped in her warmth, we feel the pull,
Of azure dreams and the ocean's lull.

As dawn approaches, the mist begins to fade,
Leaving behind the sweet masquerade.
Yet memories linger of the night's sweet balm,
In the selkie's embrace, we find our calm.

Whispers of the Seafoam Nest

In twilight's grace, the waves do sigh,
Soft murmurs rise where seabirds fly.
From coral cradles, secrets swell,
In salt-kissed breezes, tales to tell.

Frothy lace on the ocean's gown,
Cradles dreams, like treasures drowned.
With every tide, a new heart beats,
In seafoam nests, where wonder meets.

As moonlight dances on the waves,
The world transforms, the night enslaves.
Fragrant whispers ride the tide,
In sea's embrace, our hopes reside.

Beneath the stars, old spirits roam,
In every shell, a slice of home.
With gentle lap and soft caress,
The sea's own heart, forever blessed.

So listen close, where waters play,
And find the dreams that drift away.
For every echo, a story spins,
In whispers where the sea begins.

Secrets Beneath the Driftwood Canopy

Beneath the boughs where shadows dwell,
Lies a world of secrets, hard to tell.
In twisted roots, and bark of grey,
Driftwood whispers lead the way.

Nestled deep in a mossy bed,
Where forest spirits gently tread.
With every breeze, the leaves confide,
Tales of magic that never hide.

Amidst the clutter of nature's craft,
Lies a history that's deftly daft.
A tapestry woven with threads of gold,
In the quiet woods, the past unfolds.

In dappled light, where fairies dance,
Moments weave a fleeting chance.
To find the hidden, one must believe,
In all the wonders, the woods conceive.

So pause a while by the gnarled tree,
And let your heart roam wild and free.
For every branch holds a glimmer of fate,
In secrets wrapped, don't hesitate.

Enchanted Shadows of Salty Breezes

Where shadows stretch and daylight fades,
The sea's sweet song in silence wades.
Each salty breeze, a soft caress,
Encircling dreams, a tender press.

With azure waves, the horizon calls,
In whispered tones, the evening falls.
Touch the dusk as the stars ignite,
And let the night wrap you tight.

In echoes soft where seagrass sways,
The ancients speak of bygone days.
Each gentle sigh spills secrets wise,
On whispered winds beneath dark skies.

Amidst the shadows, laughs the tide,
A playful muse, with time as guide.
In every shadow, a story waits,
Where salty breezes alter fates.

So heed the call of the nightly breeze,
In the depths of dreams, find your ease.
For in the light of the moon's embrace,
Lay enchanted paths, your heart must trace.

Echoes of Dappled Dreams

In dappled light where wishes bloom,
Soft echoes carry through the room.
Each whispered thought, a seed to sow,
In fields where fragrant blossoms grow.

With colors bright and shadows cast,
Moments linger, they slip past.
Where time holds hands with fading light,
And dreams take flight into the night.

Each echo sings of laughter's past,
In every heartbeat, a spell is cast.
With gentle sighs, the forest breathes,
In the still of night, the spirit weaves.

So linger near, in twilight's hand,
Let dreams unfold, like grains of sand.
For in the heart's deep, quiet seams,
Are woven threads of dappled dreams.

Embrace the glow of starlit skies,
Where every twinkle holds surprise.
In the stillness, the echoes gleam,
Awakening the sweetest dream.

The Language of Pebbles and Waves

In whispers soft, the pebbles speak,
Their tales are old, yet far from meek.
With every crash, the waves reply,
A song of tides beneath the sky.

Each stone a story, each wave a dream,
In liquid laughter, they swirl and gleam.
The shore a canvas, rugged and wild,
Where nature's brush paints each lost child.

They dance in rhythm, a timeless tune,
Under the watchful eyes of the moon.
Harmony born in the ocean's embrace,
Pebbles and waves in a waltz through space.

Together they tell of journeys far,
Of ships that sailed beneath a star.
Echoes of laughter, whispers of pain,
In every splash, a love to gain.

The sands bear witness to fleeting grace,
As nature's flow carves each soft face.
With every pulse of the deep blue sea,
The language of life flows wild and free.

Fragments of Oceanic Reverie

Each dawn the ocean sighs anew,
A chorus of dreams in shades of blue.
The horizon stretches, a canvas bright,
Where daybreak spills its golden light.

Shells whisper secrets, lost and found,
In curls and curves, their tales abound.
Fragments of stories, the past relayed,
Through time and tide, their echoes played.

The gulls wheel overhead, in dialogue free,
With the gentle caress of the salt-kissed breeze.
Their cries linger soft on the salted air,
As the ocean sways, always aware.

In shimmering depths, where shadows dwell,
The heart of the ocean holds its swell.
With every ripple, a dream takes flight,
In fragments scattered, hidden from sight.

As twilight falls, the waves compose,
A lullaby where tranquil flows.
Night wraps the coast in silken embrace,
While whispered reveries dance and trace.

Dawn's Brush on Silken Waters

With dawn's first light, the waters gleam,
A silken veil, a waking dream.
The sun dips low with a gentle sigh,
Painting the sea, a canvas high.

Ripples echo in soft refrain,
Each pulse a promise, devoid of pain.
The horizon blushes in hues of fire,
As day awakens, hearts aspire.

Whispers on the waves, secrets unfold,
In the tender light, new stories told.
Silken waters cradle hopes anew,
As the world stirs, kissed by dew.

Mirrored skies dance on the waves' embrace,
With every ripple, a heart finds its place.
The dawn's brush paints both dream and fate,
In strokes of wonder, we celebrate.

Let the breeze carry wishes afar,
As sunlight bathes the waking tide's spar.
In each soft lap of the gentle sea,
Dawn's magic sings—forever free.

Rhythm of the Wind's Caress

The wind whispers secrets through the trees,
In symphonic dance, it rides the breeze.
With every gust, it sweeps the land,
A playful spirit, a guiding hand.

It carries tales from realms unseen,
From mountain tops to valleys green.
A lullaby born in nature's breath,
In its embrace, we conquer death.

Across the meadows, wildflowers sway,
In harmony, they dance and play.
The rhythm calls to hearts that yearn,
For every twist, a lesson learned.

Bright clouds gather, a storm might brew,
Yet in the chaos, the calm shines through.
The wind's caress, both fierce and kind,
Leads us onward, unconfined.

Embrace the whispers, both soft and bold,
For in each sound, a truth unfolds.
With every breath, let your spirit soar,
To the wind's rhythm, forevermore.

Whispers of Seafoam Dreams

In twilight's embrace, the sea does sigh,
Waves cradle secrets as they drift and fly.
Stars twinkle softly, the moon's gentle glow,
Casting whispers of dreams in the ebb and flow.

Shells tell tales of adventures past,
With grains of sand, their memories last.
The ocean's breath holds magic untold,
As hearts find solace in stories bold.

Beneath the surf, where the mermaids play,
Echoes of laughter dance with the spray.
Through currents and tides, the dreams take flight,
As seafoam weaves wonders in the night.

Silent seas shimmer with the dawn's light,
Awakening hope in the softest sight.
Each wave a promise, each ripple a song,
Whispers of seafoam where dreams belong.

And when shadows stretch as the sun starts to wane,
The ocean calls softly, never in vain.
With each gentle roll, the heart finds its piece,
In whispers of dreams, there lingers a peace.

Silhouettes of Tidal Light

As evening descends, silhouettes align,
The tide pulls the shore like a lover's design.
Moonbeams glisten on water's deep chest,
While shadows of night weave tales in their rest.

Far across the waves, stars shimmer and wink,
Guiding the lost to the safe shores they'd seek.
The whispers of light in the salt-kissed air,
Illuminate pathways that lead everywhere.

Mysteries unfurl in the softest embrace,
Carried by currents, the dreams leave no trace.
In the depths, where silence sways like a song,
Tidal light dances, where shadows belong.

Each tide that kisses the sand so sweet
Holds stories of love and of bittersweet.
In the night's gentle lap, the heart learns to fight,
To find solace in shadows and silhouettes bright.

As dawn breaks anew, colors burst wide,
The sun rises high on the ocean's tide.
With silhouettes fading, but hope glows inside,
In every wave's rhythm, our energies bide.

The Lullaby of Driftwood

Amidst the waves, the driftwood lies,
Once vibrant trees, now a soft disguise.
Sculpted by time, by the sun and the sea,
Each piece tells a story of who it might be.

In the hush of the night, the ocean hums low,
A lullaby sweet, like a warm summer glow.
The driftwood listens, as secrets unfold,
Of journeys begun and of treasures untold.

Starlight flickers on each weathered grain,
Every knot a memory, every curve a pain.
But in the soft sand, love flourishes too,
As waves sing to driftwood, renewing the view.

With gentle caress, the tide holds it near,
In hope and in laughter, in joy and in fear.
For driftwood remembers the whispers of dreams,
In lullabies crooned by the ocean's soft beams.

So let every piece that the water has claimed,
Reflect life's journey, unbroken, untamed.
In the heart of the night, may you find your own way,
Through the lullaby sung by the waves at play.

Echoes Beneath the Ocean's Veil

In the depths where the shadows embrace the light,
Echoes of whispers take flight in the night.
With the grace of the currents, they swirl and they twine,
Binding hearts to the rhythm of the sea's gentle line.

Beneath the vast ceiling of cerulean dreams,
The ocean unfolds its magnificent themes.
Each bubble that rises carries tales from below,
Of mermaids and sailors, and of love's ebb and flow.

The chorus of waves sings a haunting refrain,
Lifting spirits and joys, washing away every pain.
In the swell of the tides, the echoes remain,
Painting stories on canvas of salt and of grain.

Through crystalline waters, where sunlight shall weave,
Life dances in motion, for all who believe.
In the hush of the sea, in the whisper of breeze,
Echoes beneath the veil bring hearts to their knees.

And as twilight beckons the stars to arise,
The ocean keeps secrets, reflected in eyes.
In the arms of the night, where dreams softly sail,
Lie echoes of wonder beneath the ocean's veil.

Worn Petals on a Sandy Shore

Worn petals drift upon the sand,
Stories whispered by the tide's hand.
Each color fading under the sun,
Nostalgia woven, their journey begun.

Soft waves caress the weary blooms,
Time cradles them amidst their dooms.
A dance of memories, once so bright,
Now embraced by the approaching night.

Footprints left by dreamers dear,
Echoes linger but soon disappear.
The horizon beckons, a fading glow,
While shadows whisper of what we know.

Each petal, a fragment of a tale,
Under the watch of the moon's pale veil.
Dreams carried far on the salty breeze,
Finding solace where the heart finds ease.

Worn petals gather, now a treasure,
Adorned by sorrows, a hidden pleasure.
Their journey long, but worth the flight,
Forever cherished in the gentle night.

Serene Wands of Twilight

Serene wands beneath the veil,
Whispering secrets in the twilight pale.
They dance softly with the fading light,
Casting spells in the hush of night.

Branches stretch with a gentle grace,
The starlit sky, a shimmering lace.
With every flick, they summon dreams,
From the depths of ancient streams.

Moonbeams linger, a touch so sweet,
As magic weaves around our feet.
In this twilight, all hearts align,
Under the gaze of the grand design.

The nightingale sings her lullaby,
While the soft winds carry a sigh.
In the stillness, the world holds its breath,
Embracing the lull of quiet death.

Serene wands, with their gentle sway,
Guide us home at the close of day.
In their embrace, we find our way,
Lost in the dream of a twilight play.

Beneath Coral Skies

Beneath coral skies, the seagulls cry,
Whispers of freedom as they fly high.
Waves dance gently on the golden shore,
Each moment savored, we yearn for more.

The world ignites in a blush of hue,
A canvas stretching, so vast and new.
Pirouetting clouds in a warm embrace,
Time stands still in this sacred space.

Footprints linger on the warm, wet sand,
Tales of travelers touched by the land.
In the distance, the sun dips low,
Reminding hearts that love can grow.

Breath of salty air fills the lungs,
Songs of the ocean, forever sung.
As night approaches, we gather near,
Under the coral, we shed our fear.

Beneath coral skies, we find our truth,
In the magic of twilight, we renew our youth.
Dreams take flight on the wings of the night,
Wrapped in the colors that feel so right.

The Gentle Embrace of Luna

The gentle embrace of Luna's light,
Bathes the world in silvery white.
A soothing touch for weary souls,
Unraveling fears as her magic unfolds.

Stars gather close in her radiant glow,
While secrets of the night softly flow.
In quiet corners, shadows hum,
A lullaby known to all who come.

With every gaze, hearts begin to mend,
As dreams weave together, their threads extend.
In the stillness, we hear her call,
A promise made that we will not fall.

Whispers of time drift on the breeze,
Wrapped in her warmth, our worries cease.
In Luna's grasp, we're forever bound,
In this sacred circle, love is found.

Her light cascades, a celestial stream,
Guiding our hearts toward the unseen dream.
The world melts away, and we find grace,
In the gentle embrace of Luna's face.

Tangles of Kelp in Soft Currents

In the depths where shadows play,
Tangles sway with grace in the bay.
Whispers weave through strands so green,
A secret world, serene and unseen.

Bubbles rise like dreams set free,
An echoing song of the ancient sea.
Fish dart through the leafy maze,
In a dance of light, they twist and graze.

Currents hum with a gentle tune,
While the vastness cradles the silver moon.
Twilight spills its golden light,
Over tangled hearts, a wondrous sight.

Kelp sways softly, a lullaby,
As the tides breathe deep with a sigh.
In each swish and sway, a tale unfolds,
Of ocean's magic, whispered and told.

Memory of Dunes and Dreams

Beneath the sun where shadows dance,
The dunes drift in a timeless trance.
Whispers of sand in the wind's embrace,
Carry secrets of a forgotten place.

Footsteps fade in the golden hour,
As dreams bloom like a desert flower.
Memory melds with the ocean's roar,
Waves of longing upon the shore.

Ghosts of wanderers lost in the night,
Painted skies with shades of twilight.
Each grain of sand a story to tell,
Of hopes soaring high and wishes that fell.

Echos of laughter blend with the breeze,
Where the sun-kissed waters meet the trees.
The dance of the dunes, a timeless waltz,
Cradling dreams with no faults.

Cascade of Pearls and Twilight

In twilight's glow, pearls fall like rain,
A cascade of wishes, sweet refrain.
Luminescent droplets trace the air,
Spinning tales of hope and prayer.

Each pearl a moment, glistening bright,
Mirroring dreams in the deepening night.
They tumble and glide in a silken stream,
Resonating softly with a silvery gleam.

Time drifts gently on this shimmering tide,
As secrets of dusk and dawn coincide.
The ocean sighs with a whispering tune,
While night ascends like a silvery moon.

In the shadows, the pearls begin to swirl,
Telling stories of every boy and girl.
Each wave a heartbeat, a rhythm so sweet,
With the cadence of twilight, their melody meets.

Tranquil Spirits in Drifted Realms

In drifted realms where whispers dwell,
Tranquil spirits weave a gentle spell.
Beneath the stars sparkling like dew,
They gather around, shimmering and blue.

Threads of dreams weave through the night,
Guiding the lost with their soft light.
Each heart that wanders, drawn near by grace,
Finds solace in this enchanted space.

Echoes of laughter float in the air,
In the quiet, they linger, tender and rare.
With every sigh from the winds that cool,
Spirits dance in a mystical pool.

Beneath the boughs of ancient trees,
They whisper secrets on the breeze.
In this tranquil dance, the past melds anew,
A tapestry woven in every hue.

www.ingramcontent.com/pod-product-compliance
Ingram Content Group UK Ltd.
Pitfield, Milton Keynes, MK11 3LW, UK
UKHW021440290125
4349UKWH00039B/557

9 781805 644385